SOMAT(IC) --- The Fall – 2017

The purpose of this document is to declare the philosophical / social / and cultural stance that The Primitive Entertainment Workshop is choosing to take in our current socio-political environment.

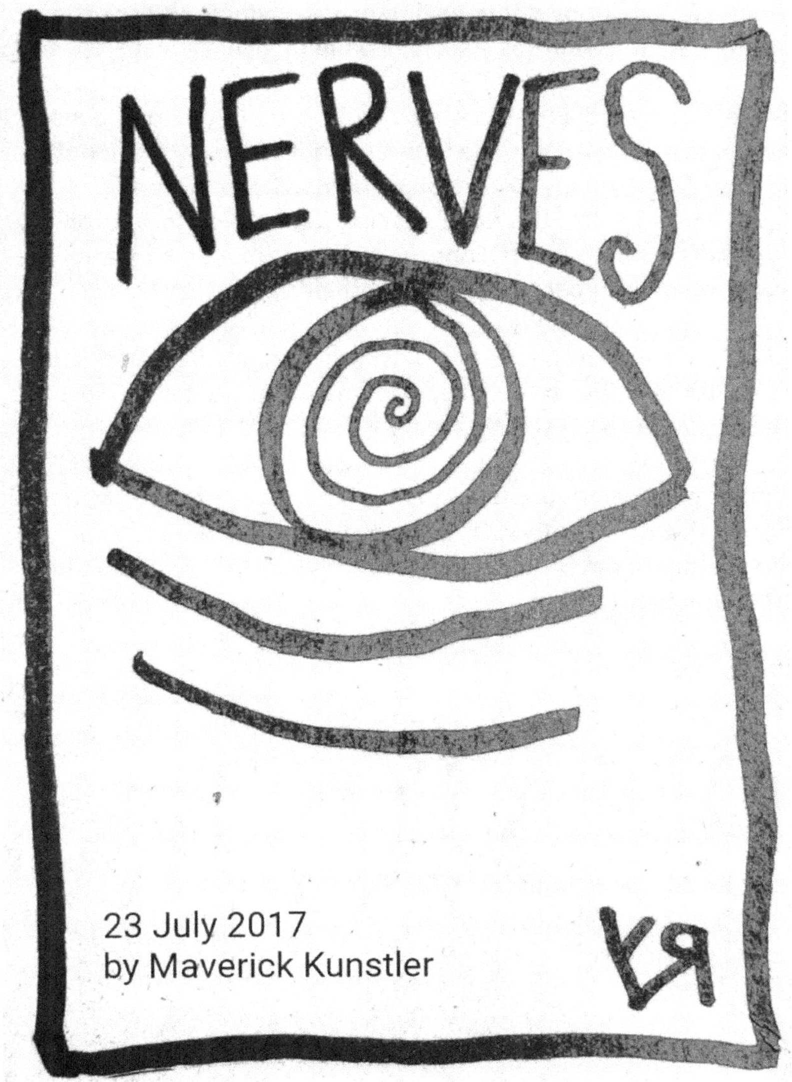

NERVES

23 July 2017
by Maverick Kunstler

(Artwork by Yggdrasil R. Rouser, PPT.)

The products that we buy: phones and computers and televisions, have become mobile prisons, cages that enthrall our minds. We will halt our own trains of thought---our personal ideas---to answer the beep and call of our electronic distractions. We spend countless hours watching cat videos and reality t.v. and living in endless empty fictional universes---but we don't know our own friends or families anymore. (Clicking a "like" button isn't the same as shaking a hand or giving a hug.)

Meanwhile, social media has become a tempestuous, heinous, echo chamber. People who believe the GOP / Republican agenda see nothing but streams of GOP / Republican leaning media. Democrats and (supposed) liberals suffer the same near-sightedness, absorbing only materials that reinforce and bolster their own positions, but without any counterpoint argument ever crossing their sight.

FAKE NEWS! It's become a joke and a nightmare and a battle cry. Our reality t.v. obsession has now spilled over into REAL politics. We are living the NETWORK EXECUTIVE fantasy. IT'S ALL T.V. NOW!

What I'm proposing with this document is a new way of thinking, a new means of coping with the FAKENESS of fake news and the ECHOES of the echo chamber effect. This is an operations-manual for you brain, brought to you by:

THE SCHOOL OF MADNESS AS TRUTH (INNER CIRCLE)

SOMAT(IC)

President: Dr. Maverick Kunstler, PPT
Vice President: Allen Winterhaven
Sergeant at Arms: Alice Traveler, WFC
Minister of Propaganda: Yggdrasil R. Rouser, PPT

Copywrong: 2017
In conjunction with:

The Primitive Entertainment Workshop
https://primitiveentertainment.wordpress.com/

Electric Boogaloo

Addiction to stimulation. Are we living in the Matrix? Has it GOT us? I'm sitting at a coffee table, uncomfortably, typing into a machine. I can see what's on the screen. I watch it change as I type, and erase, and retype, and I wonder if what's up there is really making any sense---and then I realize that, for the first time since Club Dada in the early 1900s, making sense is no longer necessary. Does the president of the USA make any sense? Not a bit. Does sending messages to a person sitting next to you on the couch, but not actually SPEAKING to them, make any sense? No.

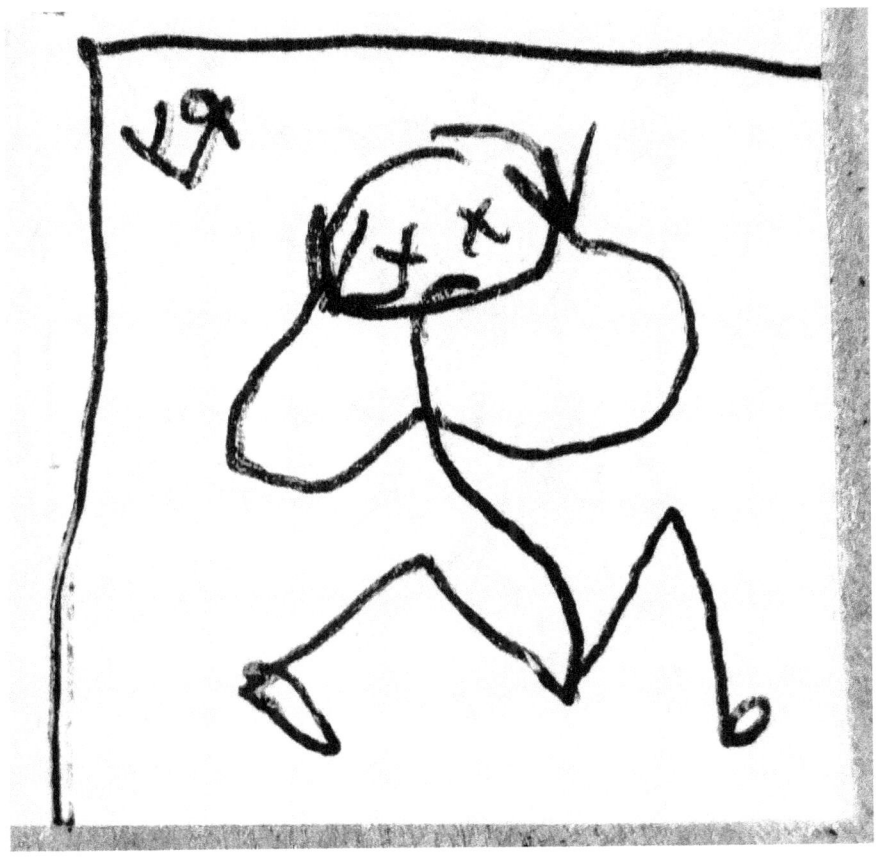

One of our cats is curled up and asleep on a vintage videogame system. Doesn't seem like it would be very comfortable to me. Cords everywhere. Makes walking hazardous, even in my own living room!

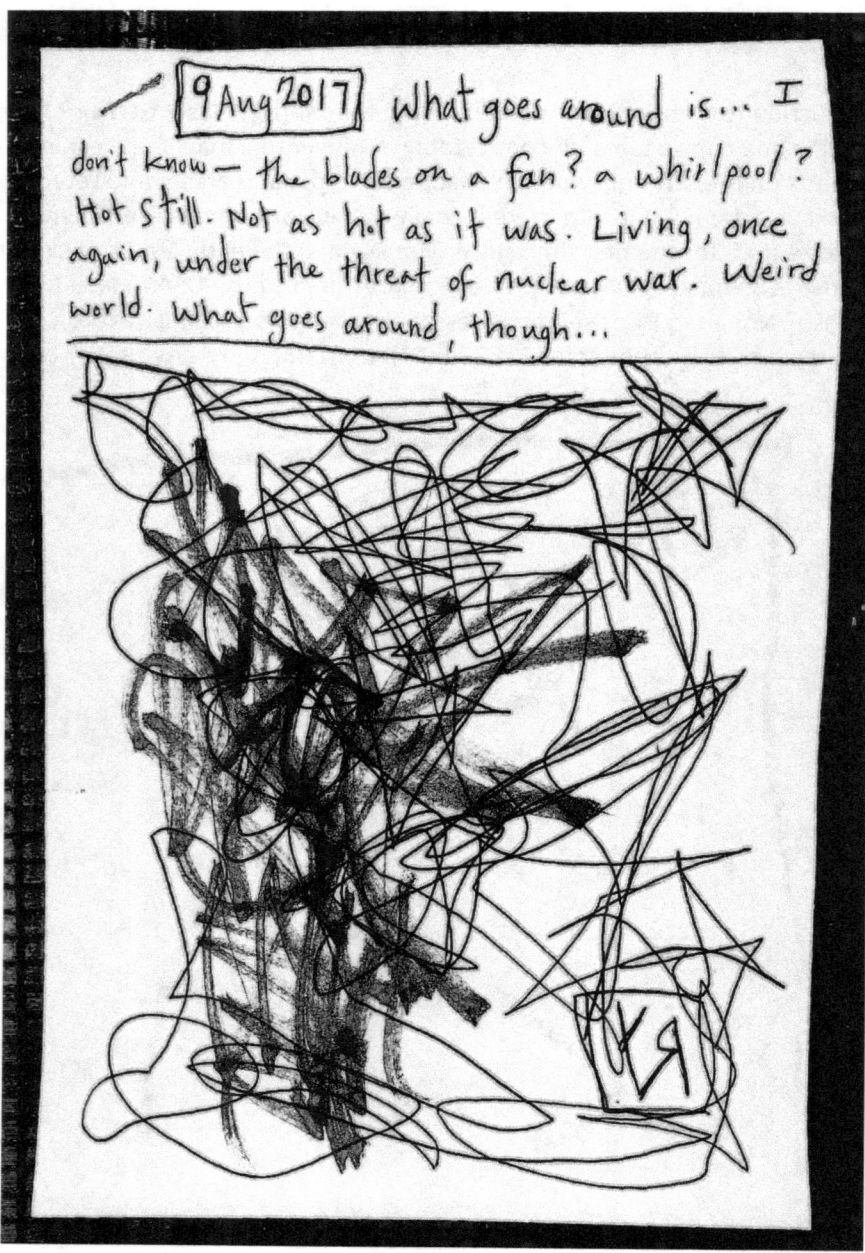

Rust in my blood... I still remember the last nuclear scare. My mom wouldn't let me watch the movie, *The Morning After*, because it was too terrifyingly possible. More boom? Let them fly? Is it all okay?

"The People Need to Know!" by Richard F. Yates

I stopped by the editor's office, but I didn't have an appointment. I said, "Goddam it! The people need to know about this!!!"

The editor, sniffing a possible story, smiled, "Of course! What do you know about this heinous affair!?" He waved towards a chair in front of his desk, but I stood my ground.

"First, they stopped making my favorite frozen, breaded, chicken breast strips!" I said, and the man gasped. "And have you tried to get those little red chimichanga meals lately? Impossible! It's criminal! And where are all the Chewy Sweet-Tarts? AND, some sick individuals went and changed the formula for Trix cereal, like twenty times! It's not even the same damn cereal anymore!" I slammed my fist on his desk. He wiped a tear from his eye.

"My God," he said and crossed himself. "I had no idea how bad it had gotten out there. I'm isolated here in my Media Palace... I haven't shopped in months."

I gritted my teeth, even though the dentist told me that was bad, and stared the man down. He didn't grasp the full problem. "Last time I went to Target," I practically growled, "they had stopped making my regular cut of pants. I'm a thicker guy with very short legs. Do you know how hard it is to find pants that fit me that are comfortable...?"

And then I saw it. His facial expression changed. He looked lost for a second, then angry, then like he'd popped a button off his shirt. I nodded. He finally UNDERSTOOD.

"What can we do? How can we stop this?" he said. He started to sob.

"We need to let the people know. It's up to US to save everyone from a fate worse than death," I said.

He was shaking his head. "I can't... I can't... I'm not strong enough. The advertisers... they'll know!"

I came around the desk and shook him by the shoulders. I would have slapped him, but he had mustard on his cheek.

"Get a grip, Hensley!" I said, sternly.

"My name is Hicks..." he said in a weak voice.

"Not anymore, Hensley! You're under my protection now, so I get to decide what your name is!" His eyes grew wide, and he pushed a button on his desk.

"Yes, Mr. Hensley?" an older, female voice said.

"Get me a T.V. guide and a bag of pepperoni sticks. I've got some work to do..." He pushed the button again and then said "beep," which I guess turned the intercom off. "As soon as I finish the crossword puzzle I'll start dismantling the entire global economic corporate system." He still sounded worried, but I was certain he could do it.

"Save one of those pepperoni sticks for me. I'll be back on Thursday to see how you're doing. Meanwhile, I'm going to Smacky Joe's Pizza to play Ms. Pacman." I gave him a thumbs-up then dove for the office door. Hensley was on board. Only sixty-four billion more people to go and we'll save this goddam world!

[**NOT** the end...(Only the beginning...) But probably the end.]

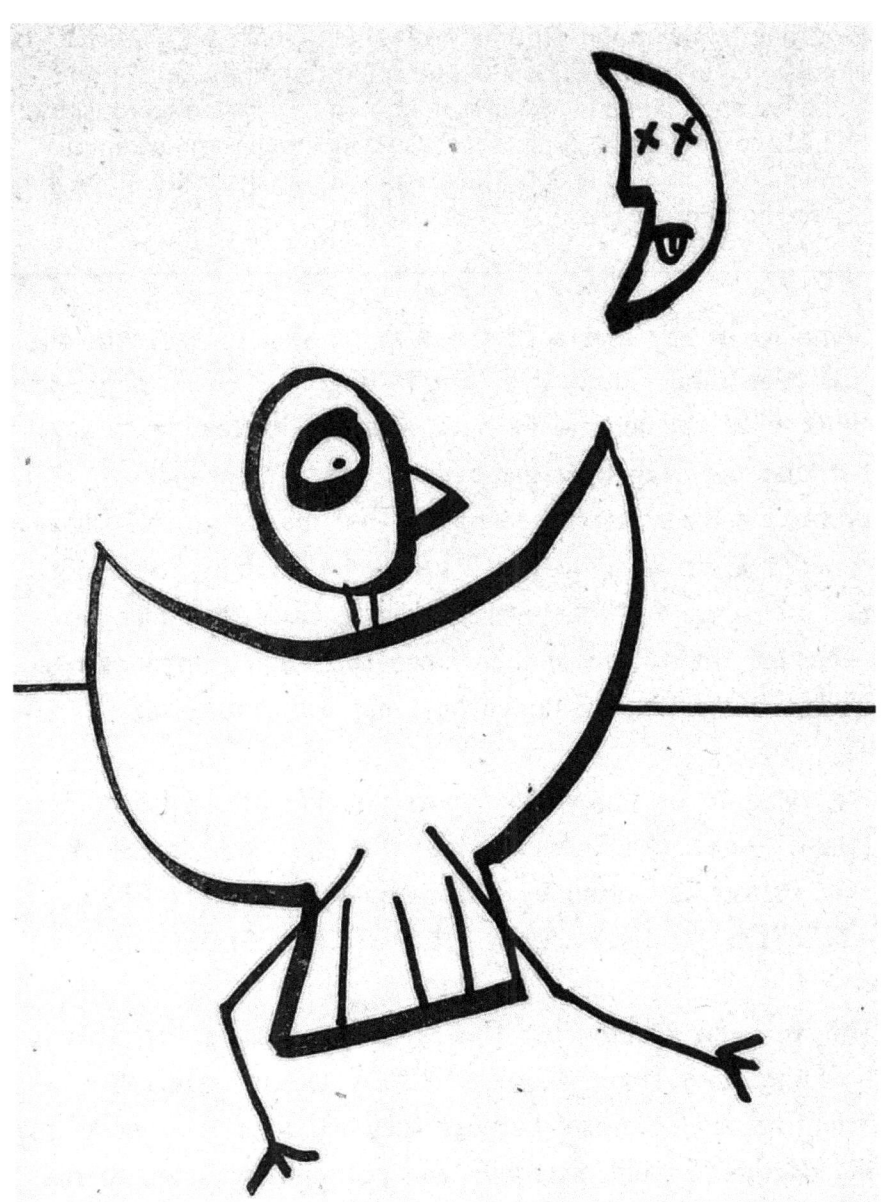

"Birdman Escapes into the Night!"

By drugging the moon, Birdman was able to make his escape. He'd stolen every good idea that he could find at the local library and even photocopied a dollar bill, knowing it was dangerous, but he liked to live on the edge. Let those coppers just try to capture him again! Now that he knew about the salt on the tail-feathers bit, he was home free!

Some might say that a person with nothing to say should just keep their mouth shut, but I disagree. I would argue that VERY FEW people actually have anything interesting to say, but that they say their garbage in such a slick and professional way that people go, "That makes sense!" (Make America Great Again!) So... FUCK IT! If they can spout that nonsense (without ever explaining HOW they plan on executing their slogans) then I can spout my own nonsense, which isn't pretending to be anything BUT nonsense.

I'm trying to be funny. ALL of us are. We KNOW (like Hensley does, like Birdman does) that the world is full of shit. History is written by historians---but NOBODY PAYS ATTENTION TO THEM, EVEN THOUGH THEY SHOULD!!!!

They've been warning us: This is how fascism starts. This is how theocracy starts. Didn't ANYBODY watch Brazil??? Scientists are scientists because they did their homework. So did doctors. So did historians and economists. Listen to the fucking experts. Don't be a dumbass! Entertainers, like me, are where you get nonsense. Remember that...

SOMAT(IC)

SOMAT(IC)

SOMAT(IC)

Somat(ic)

SOMAT(IC)

SOMAT(IC)

The funny thing about repetition is that it can often encourage belief. In other words, if you hear something said for long enough, you can start to believe it, even if you have direct evidence that whatever you're being told is complete bullshit.

SOMAT(IC)

SOMAT(IC)

There are memory experts, like Elizabeth Loftus (from the University of Washington), who have proven conclusively that people have shitty memories. You CREATE a new memory when you remember something, which means that, over time, you are actually changing the memory that you think you're remembering. (You should look up her work and read about this for yourself. It's pretty fucking amazing...)

I've got first-hand experience of this type of phenomena. I've kept a journal since I was about seven years old. (I'm 45 now, although I might not be that age anymore by the time you read this...I might not even still be around...) And, even though I thought I had a good memory, I can go back to my notes of an event that happened when I was twenty and READ EXACTLY how it happen...and it's never like I remember it..

Another example is this: your personal image of who you are changes constantly. Consider some cherished childhood memory: a favorite Christmas present or a great camping trip. Try to remember who you were then... Who do you see? Anyone? Now, go get an old photo album (those were big books with pictures in them) and look at those people? Is that who you are still?

Does any of this matter? Sort of.

Write shit down. Write a letter. If you have a favorite text message or email from somebody, print it out. You WON'T remember it. Not unless you take the time to INTENTIONALLY remember it syllable for syllable. (Most people don't do this.) Plus, if the power goes out and you can't use your laptop, you can still hold a piece of paper in your hand and read it by candle-light.

Why did I bring this up? Because Orwell was right. People are changing the facts. People are recasting history. Without his trusty (and forbidden) journal, Winston Smith would have forgotten what was real and true. Don't believe the repetitions. Keep a journal. Remember how YOU feel. Remember what is right and true...

New and improved!
Now with PEP!

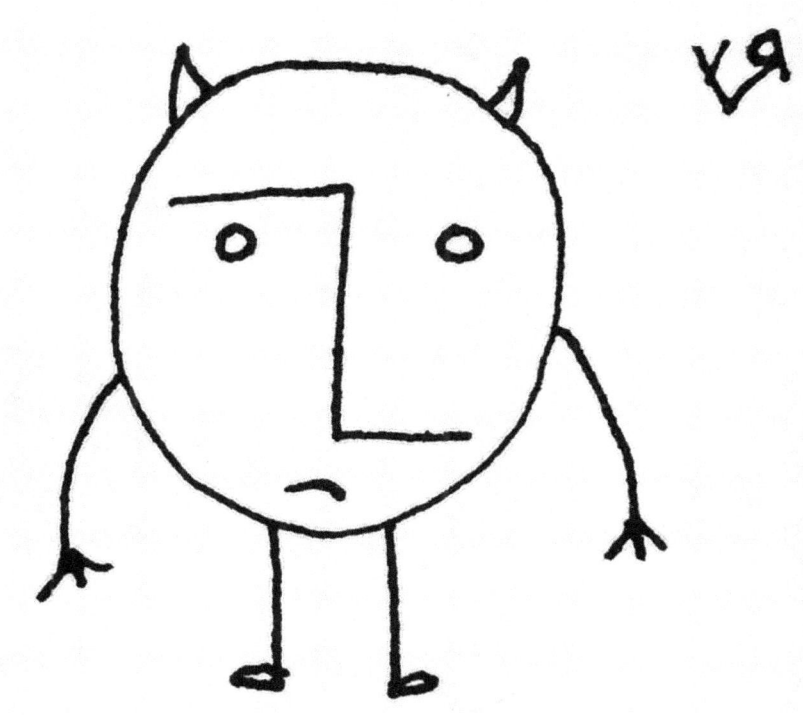

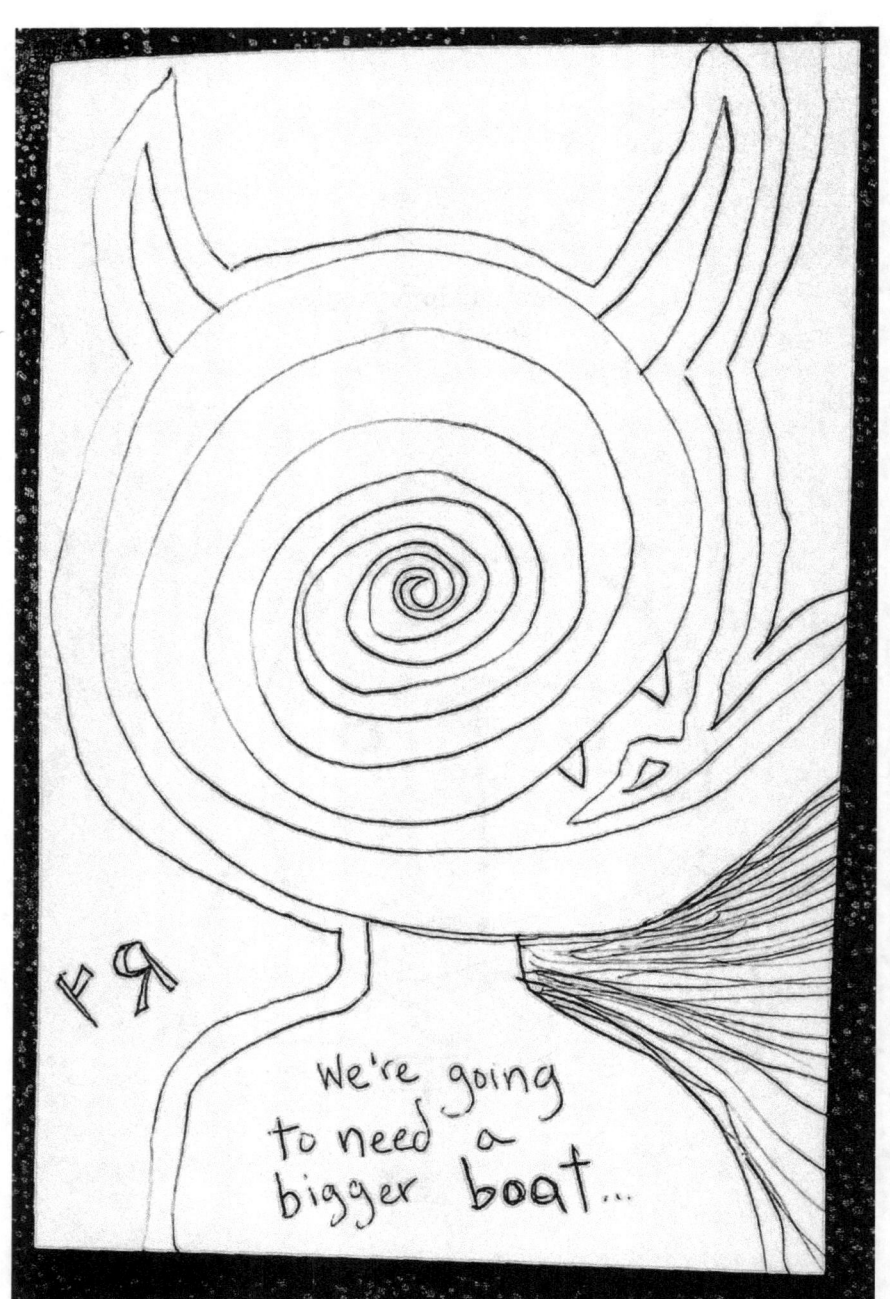

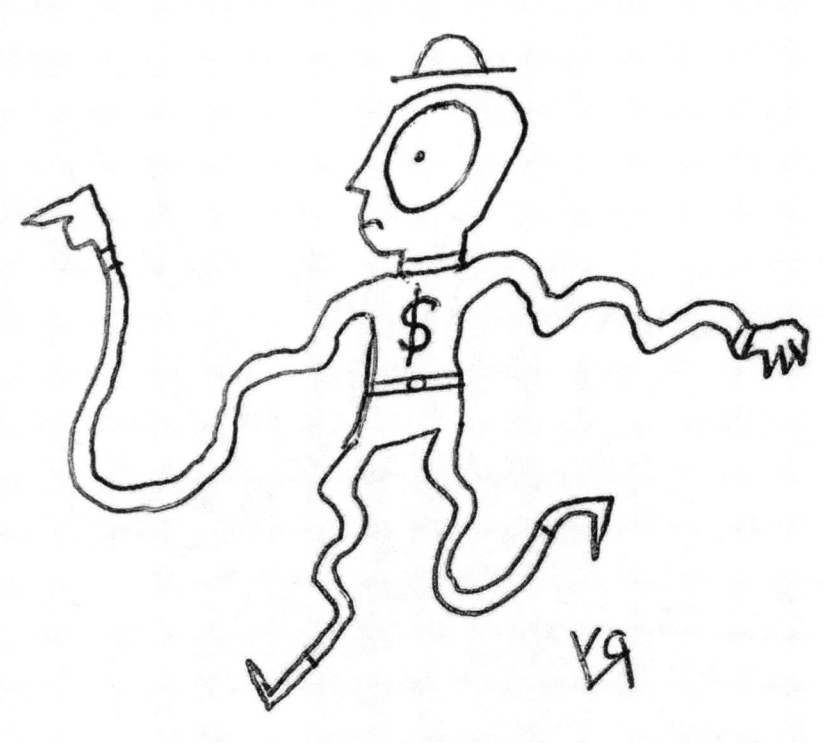

The happy consumer doesn't differentiate on his own. The happy consumer stands in line for the midnight release of the newest gadget that's going to change his life forever! The happy consumer works very hard, but he has to so that he can afford that giant t.v. and that blue-tooth surround sound system that connects with all his exciting appliances. (His refrigerator can even tell him when he's out of milk AND send a digital coupon to his phone that he can use when he goes shopping! Wonderful!)

But happy consumers are only happy until the NEXT BIG THING comes out, which makes all of the other things that they have obsolete (or, kinda "last season" anyway.) Poor little consumer.

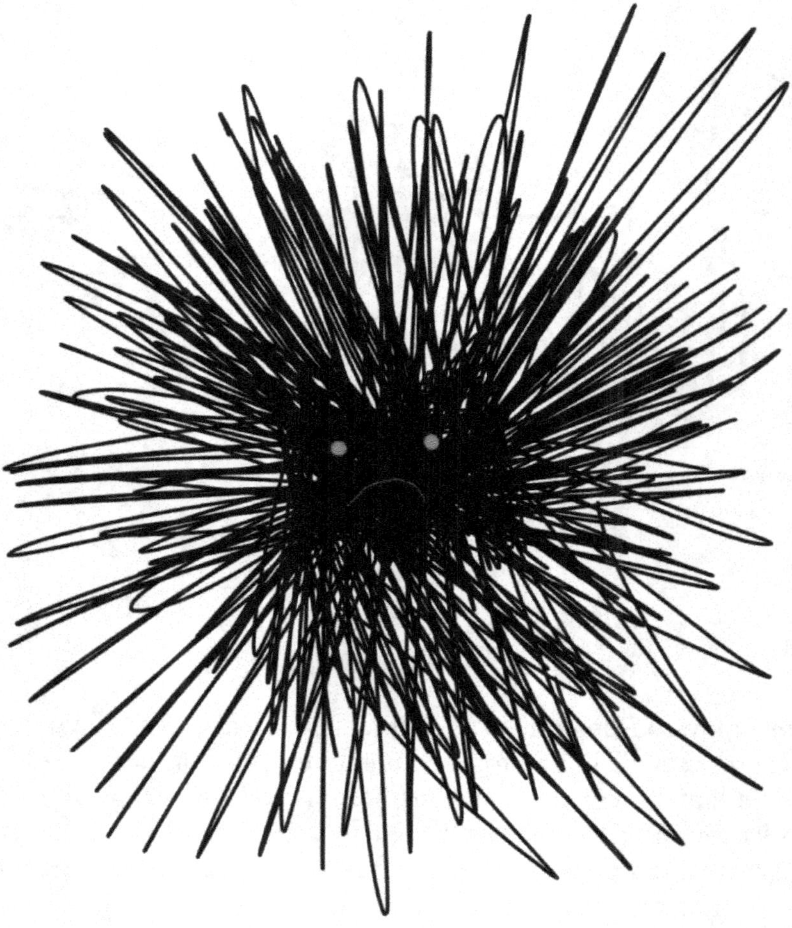

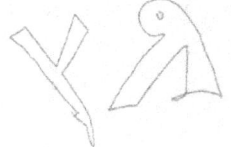

I've always wanted to start my own religion. (Not always...but for long enough.) In fact, I did start a religion once, a few years ago, and then I restarted it when I forgot the passwords for the website to the original religion. I went back to the first version and read through what a few friends of mine and I had written, and it was pretty funny---but not quite as MAGICAL as I had hoped it would be.

The second version of the religion was more fully realized, we had HOLIDAYS and everything, but it got out of hand rather quickly. It went the way of most satire religions, and got too silly for its own good, past the point where anyone could believe it.

So a good religion has to strike that fine balance between magic and believability.... The weird thing about all of this is how incredibly SILLY most of the major religions that are believed by millions of people really are. Most of them espouse some form of MAGIC, even though there isn't ANY scientifically provable evidence for the existence of magic in the world at all. NONE. Zip. So all those miracles and supernatural creatures that fill up all those other religions---just silly.

BUT PEOPLE BELIEVE... Why????

My guess is that they just feel HELPLESS, and they want to believe someTHING is in charge and working for their benefit. (It's not true, but it's what they want.)

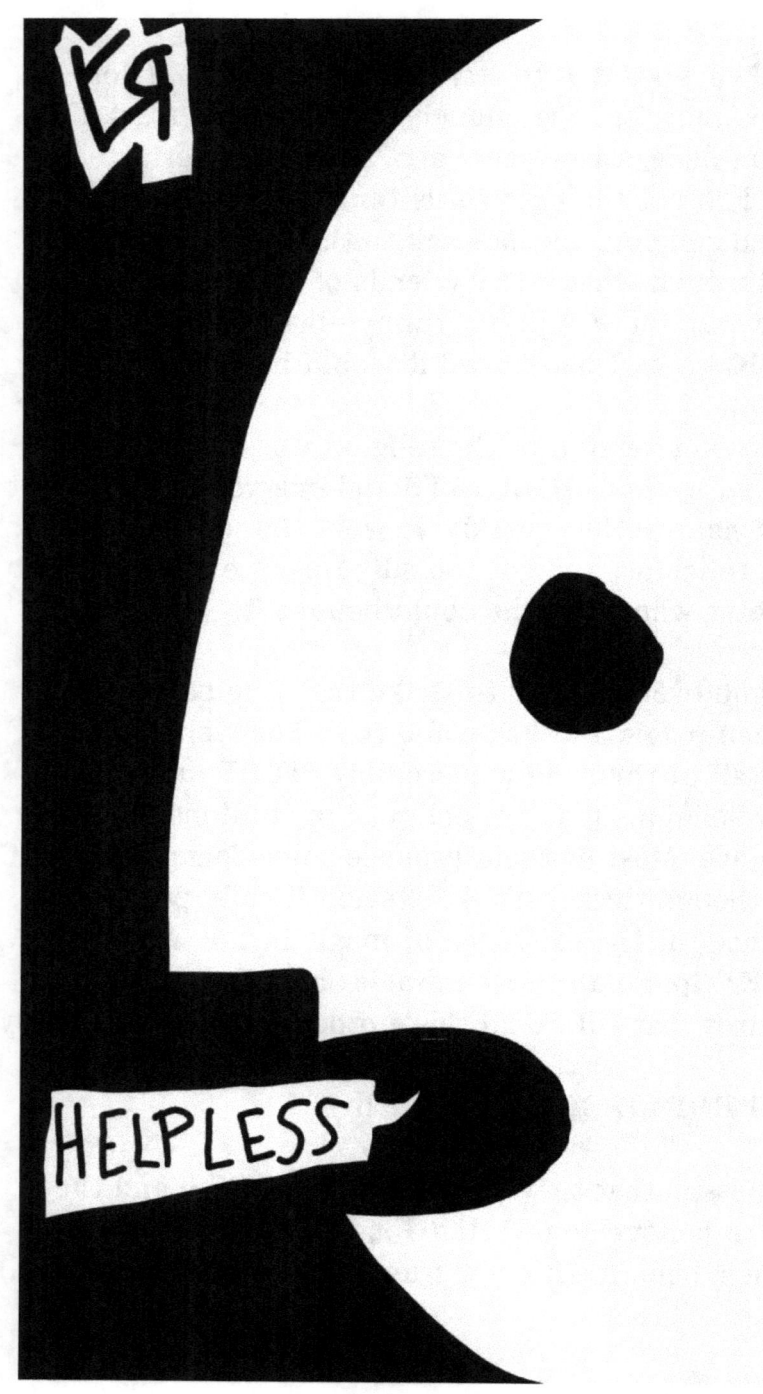

"Jerry's Head" (A short story with roots in soft science)

"The ghosts are all gone, so I can go home, right?" Jerry said.

"No Jerry. There were no ghosts," the doctor said. "They were all in your head. Nothing more."

"Right. No ghosts. Never were any ghosts," Jerry smiled and shook the doctor's hand. The doctor signed the papers and stood behind his desk as Jerry exited.

Jerry was quiet on the cab ride home. He'd been gone for three weeks this time. Hopefully, Janey had remembered to water his plants. The goldfish had both died the LAST TIME he was gone, so he didn't have to worry about them. (But he still did.)

The cab pulled up in front of Jerry's house. He swallowed, paid the driver, and walked toward the door, holding his bag in front of his chest like a shield.

"All in my head," he mumbled and turned the key. He pushed the door open and saw that the hallway was dark. A bulb must have burned out. He stepped across the threshold.

And a quiet voice said, "Welcome home, Jerry. We missed you…"

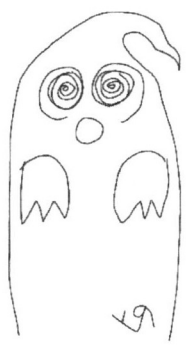

"Madness (A definition)" by M. Kunstler

Was Jerry "crazy?" He heard voices. He saw things that the doctors told him weren't there---but he EXPERIENCED these things himself. The voices may have only been in his head, but the voices WERE in his head. He wasn't wrong...

Madness, as our good buddy Foucault showed us (in a very tedious and difficult to get through book, Madness and Civilization) that each society defines its own madness. Suffering from battle fatigue (or shell shock or PTSD) to the point where a soldier goes berserk and starts killing anyone around him was considered madness during WWI, but in Viking cultures, these fierce "Berserker" fighters were revered and feared!

Eating people is considered mad, except in the many (MANY!) cultures where it was (perhaps still is) socially acceptable. Murder is mad, except when it's not. Being possessed by demons or spirits is mad, except when it's not... Being homosexual was considered a form of mental illness, even in the U.S., until people stopped being stupid. (Some people.)

Madness is situational, and in some cases, it's necessary. If the WORLD has gone crazy (as ours clearly has) then it us up to the BRAVEST of us to BECOME MAD until such time as the world stops being stupid again. The form of madness is up to you, and should be chosen for its appropriateness to situation that needs to be addressed. Fools, get ready to rush in there... GO!!!!

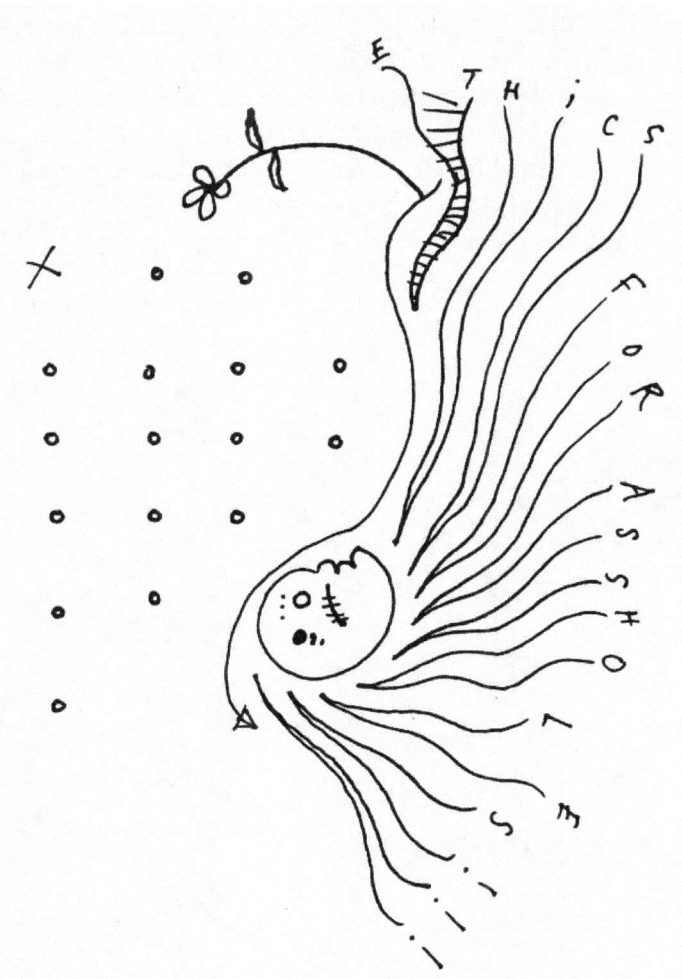

History is often chosen for it's delicious aftertaste. We caress the sides of the boat, even after we've tipped it completely over under over under over unidentified male found loitering in the sand trap at Burger Barn. The hassle that lasts is the hassle worth hustling for which that to this or then work work work work work work work work until you dieeeeee...

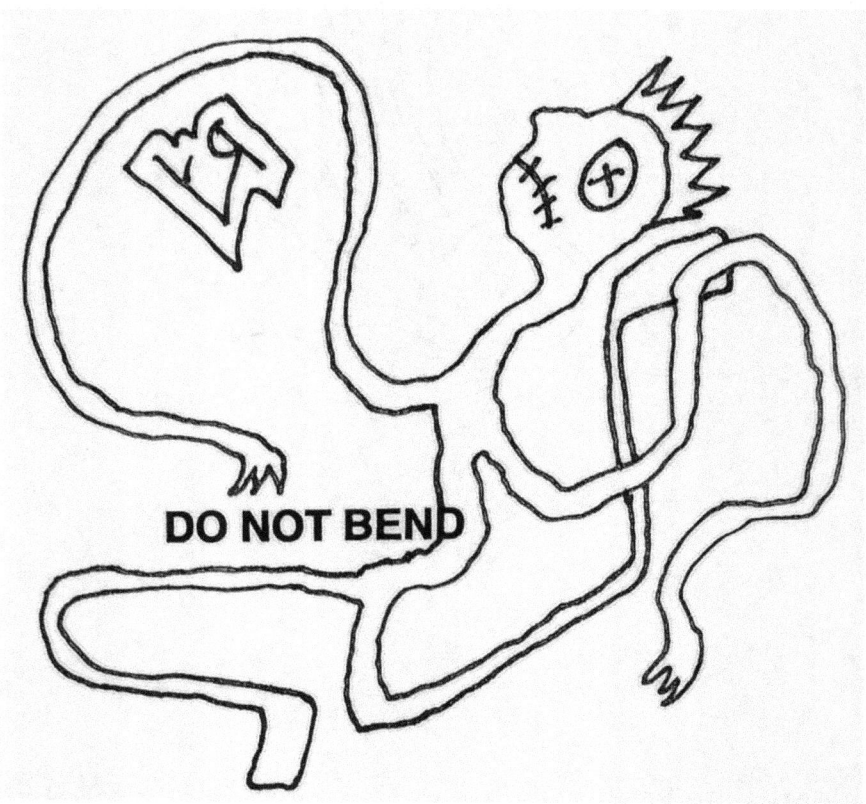

The real enemy is beneath the soil. Warm your hands in the fire in the eyes of the one you love to love you baby on board. November was going to come again, and there was nothing we could do to stop it...

"History of The Primitive Entertainment Workshop"

The P.E.W. was born on March 4th, 1797, in Milbourne, North Carolina. It's father (Harold "Mashed Potatoes" Benwold) was a hair dresser and its mother (Candice Featherstone-Benwold) was a famous astronaut. (She was, in fact, the first woman to fly a hot air balloon through a drive-thru!) Unfortunately, P.E.W.'s parents divorced several years before it was born, so it has never actually met its mother in person, but it's seen some photographs.

After attending the naval academy in Colorado Springs, Montana, P.E.W. bummed around Europe for a few days trying to find itself. Instead, it found a large bowl of mashed potatoes sitting on a park bench in Munich, and immediately took a train back to North Carolina, only to discover that its father was alive and well, though confused about how to program a VCR.

By the early 1980s, P.E.W. had become the President of the Godzilla Appreciation Society, and moonlighted as a gas can on the weekends for extra income. After a short marriage to a piece of cheesecake, P.E.W. decided to leave society entirely and moved to the Pacific Northwest, in 1991, where it's lived ever since. It now spends most of its time knitting arguments and other poisons and dipping the ends of girls' pigtails in fluorescent orange ink.

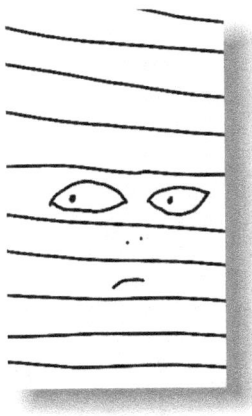

One of the Priests of Nothingness, preparing for holy communion of gas station chicken strips and soda pop… After the feast, he will wash his hands in a tub of hand sanitizer and then stand in the lawn and scream about unfair wages and chronic back pain (until the magic red and blue lights appear and he is led back into the house.)

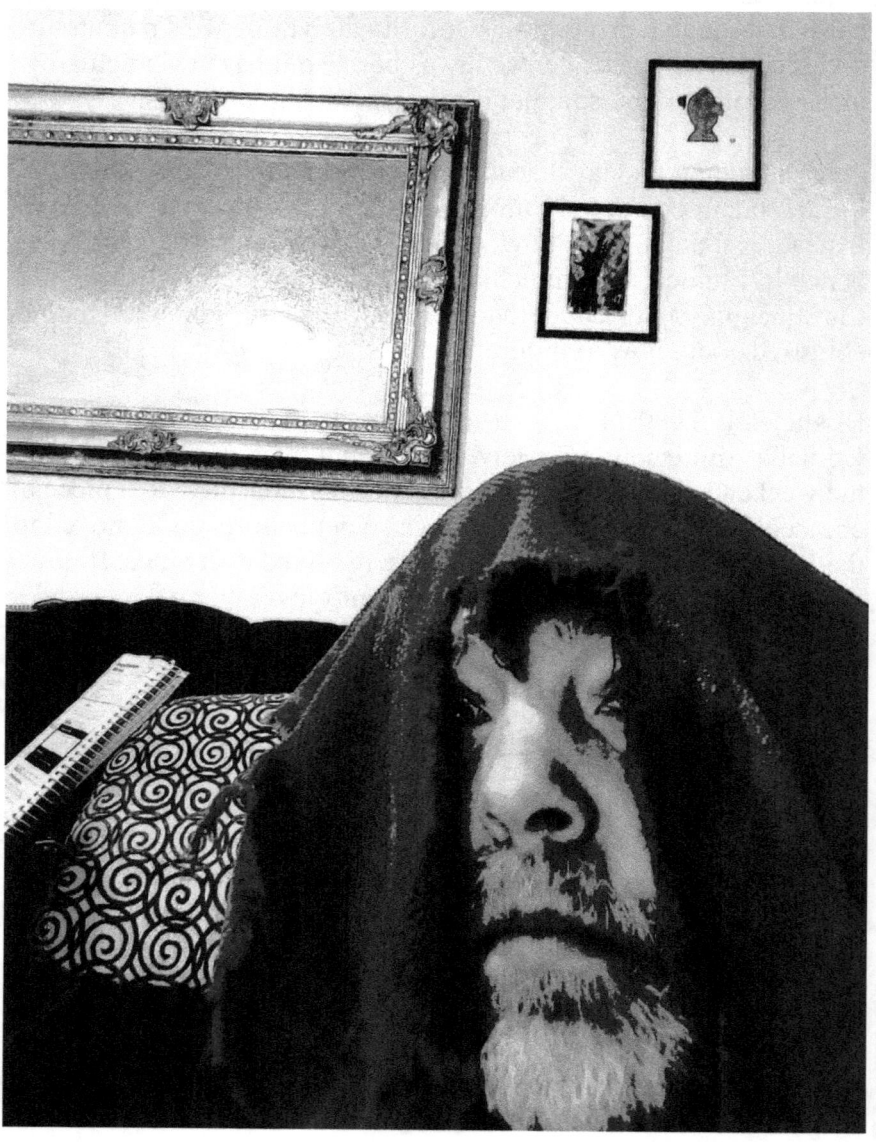

OTHER PLACES TO FIND ADVENTURE:

The Primitive Entertainment Workshop (Fictional Occurrences)
https://primitiveentertainment.wordpress.com/

SOMAT(IC) (The Official Website for the School)
https://schoolofmadnessastruth.blogspot.com/

Read a Damn Book (Book Reviews)
https://readadamnbookwithrfy.blogspot.com/

I Lost the Plot a Few Miles Back (Random Quackery)
https://ilosttheplotafewmilesback.blogspot.com/

The Museum of What I Like (Art from the real world)
https://themuseumofwhatilike.blogspot.com/

The New Church of DIM (An alternative faith)
https://thenewchurchofdim.wordpress.com/

The Two Ricks and The Neon Apocalypse (A radio show)
https://www.podomatic.com/podcasts/thetworicks

Electronic Fog (A poetry and sound-works podcast)
https://www.podomatic.com/podcasts/electronicfog

Twitter: @richardfyates

Redbubble:
https://www.redbubble.com/people/richardfyates

Deviant Art:
https://richardfyates.deviantart.com/

Ello:
https://ello.co/richardfyates

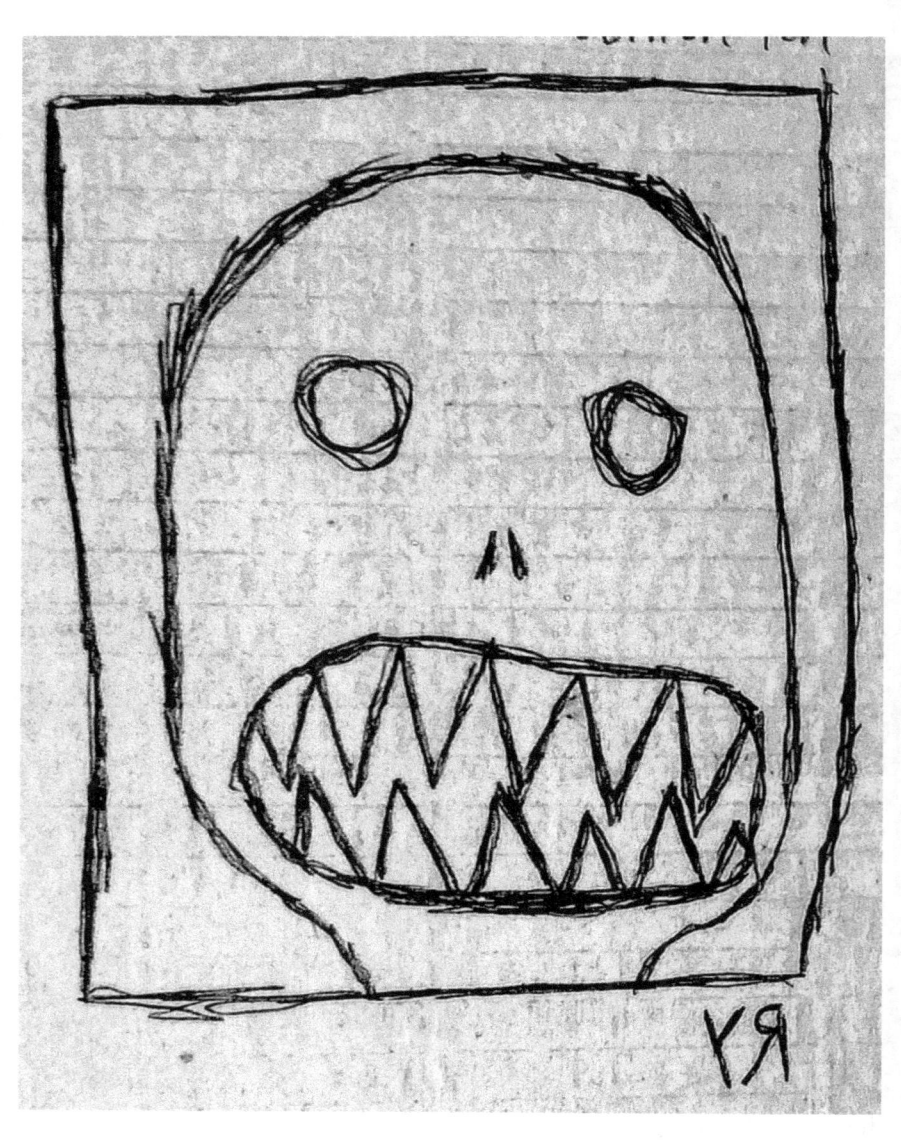

END OF LINE…

www.ingramcontent.com/pod-product-compliance
Lightning Source LLC
Chambersburg PA
CBHW071223240526
45470CB00018B/2293